Nineteen Poems
Around a Divorce
and Beyond

Kevin Arnold

Nineteen Poems
Around a Divorce
and Beyond

Kevin Arnold

APPLEGATE VALLEY PUBLISHING
Grants Pass, Oregon

Copyright © 2010 by Kevin Arnold

First Print Edition 2010

No part of this publication may be reproduced by any mechanical, photographic recording or electronic process or in the form of a photographic recording, no may it be stored in a retrieval system, transmitted or otherwise copied for public or private use without prior written permission from the author.

ISBN: 978-0-9827759-0-5

Library of Congress Control Number: 2010910688

To contact the publisher write:

Applegate Valley Publishing
510 Copper Drive
Grants Pass, Oregon 97527
541-862-7021
email: ApplegateValleyPublishing@gmail.com

Front Cover: Oil Painting, "Love and Loss Are The Same #2"
by George Oswalt
Back Cover: Oil Painting, "Love and Loss Are The Same #1"
by George Oswalt

Printed in the United States of America

Dedication

To Carol, who has helped me move beyond.

Individual Poem Dedications:

"Softball" and "Ponytail" are for Galway.

"Dreamwomen" is for H.

"How to Measure Yourself" is for Al.

"My Father's Eyes," and "Hooky" are for my father and mother.

Foreword

I published *Nineteen Poems Around a Divorce* in 1999 and sold it at readings and conferences until I ran out of copies. I've also given the book to friends who face divorce. They've consistently thanked me, saying the poems made them feel less alone. Divorce, especially with children still in the home, tends to be surrounded by guilt.

Editor Deborah Perdue suggested that I expand the nineteen with poems from other periods of my life. So after the first section, where Deb re-created the initial book, I now branch out. "Parents," may be of special interest to adult children of alcoholics. The third section, "Johnna," explores my first marriage and my relationship with our daughter. The final poems, in "Beyond," show our lives continuing after the storm.

The kids are doing well. Johnna earned her MFA from Mills in Fine Art Photography and teaches in San Francisco; Scotty is now in his second year at the Musical Theater Writing MFA program at NYU; and Kate, whose fifth-grade essay is one of the original nineteen poems, is starting her second year of medical school at Georgetown in Washington DC. Still, given the choice between going through a divorce with children and undergoing a mouthful of root canals, I'd recommend oral surgery every time.

Portola Valley, California, 2010

Table of Contents

Dedication	i
Foreword	ii
Acknowledgements	v

PART I – NINETEEN POEMS AROUND DIVORCE

Original Dedication from Earlier Book	1
Corduroy	2
Sensualand	3
Long Before Separation, Squaw Valley	5
Dreamwomen	6
Homecoming	8
Autobiographical Incident (Kate Arnold)	9
To Bo	11
Here in the Kitchen	12
How It Went	14
Separation	15
Transitions, a Trilogy	16
Ponytail	22
Divorce Albums	24
A Wave Starts as a Swell…	26
Separated	28
My Son's Sex	29
They're Sure I Was Never Young	30
A Way to Measure Yourself	32

PART 2 – JOHNNA

    Sleeping Father   37
    First Wife   38
    Early Morning, Amherst   39
    Japanese Graveyard on Kauai   41
    The Art Opening   43

PART 3 – PARENTS

    My Parents Before Me   49
    Dad's Knights   50
    Maverick   51
    Hooky   53
    My Father's Eyes   54
    Falling   56
    Harry's Songs   60
    Shaking   62
    Softball   64

PART 4 – AND BEYOND

    Free, Fly, Back, Breast   71
    Carpaccio   73
    Dancing at Halloween   74
    Invitation to the Opera   75
    At Jasper Ridge Ranch   76

ABOUT THE AUTHOR   77

Acknowledgements

I would like to thank *The Squaw Valley Community of Writers* as several of these poems were written in the summer workshops, and *Poetry Center San Jose* and those who have supported the organization with me as president for the last twelve years. A portion of the book's proceeds will be shared with these two organizations.

I would also like to acknowledge where some of these poems were previously published:

Boston Phoenix Literary Review—"Homecoming"

Dallas Opera News—"Invitation to the Opera"

eNVee—"Carpaccio" (as "Seeds")

Foothills—"Free, Fly, Back, Breast"

Mokehillian Review of Poetry—"Dancing at Halloween"

Manzanita, "At Jasper Ridge Ranch," written as part of the novel *The Sureness of Horses*, (as "At Webb Ranch")

Mudfish 6 from Lincoln Center—"Dreamwomen"

Poetsfeet 3—"Sleeping Father"

Seattle Review XV, no. 1—"Sensualand"

Sirens—"Softball"

The Clock, Desperados, and Jeremy, the first Zapizdat Review—"Maverick," and "Dad's Knights" (as "My Father on Horseback")

Visions, International—"Transitions" as "Overnight I: Transitions", and "Overnight II: Waiting for Dawn"

Writer's Market—"Falling" (excerpted)

Part 1

Nineteen Poems Around a Divorce

ORIGINAL DEDICATION FROM EARLIER BOOK

To my mother,
who made me feel special when she could,

and Clara, daughter of a bank president,
who, despite him, taught me the warmth of a
woman's love,

and Janet, who gave me Johnna
and for whom I was a continual disappointment

and the others, from near loves to curious glancers
who gave me more than I ever deserved,

and mostly to Bo, who gave me two kids and all
I am today.
She gave me the courage to be less of a man
and set my voice free: all these poems are hers.

CORDUROY

If the feminists knew
you pack my bags, Bo,
well, we won't tell them
how you always include
lotions and pajamas or,
for this trip to Seattle,
warm pants and jacket,
wide-waled corduroy,
thick peasant cloth,
so after potato salad and beer,
when I leave the bookstore,
wander down to the ferries,
the wind tries to nip at us
but it can't.

SENSUALAND

Come, you've been chosen,
down the passage between Adventureland
   and Tomorrowland,
near that stage where people eat lunch.
Yes, that's the diffident teenager from the Storyland line,
still in the v-necked t-shirt over
those small breasts,

and that compact mother from the valley,
who crisply waited for Small World with her tall son,
she is still in those white pants,
her muscles still attached
in that unexpectedly tight fashion.

The folks running things now
know Walt would turn over in his grave if he had one,
but believe to last forever you've got
to change,
so they bring interested strangers together
for a new ride, with few rules: No pain the first time. And
precautions.
Except for these,
                no saying no.
No long conversations
                    about how you got here.

(Sensualand, continued)

You probably won't see
your wife.
Perhaps on your second stay,
but they generally keep spouses apart
for their first trip to Sensualand.

Your selection by the elves wasn't random;
they are told: watch their eyes.
The standard charge to the elves is
look past the hearts,
watch the eyes.

LONG BEFORE SEPARATION, SQUAW VALLEY

Can't do it tonight.
No poems come.
Cannot bring pleasure,
except to my wife, at three a.m. when
we throw tired bodies at one another.
At that ecstatic time my soul
makes a dying-animal sound
for how lucky I am
to be here with her.

DREAMWOMEN

No eggs to protect, at home with your power
— touch me right there, now —
restore hair on my head, relax my back,
you women in my dreams —
oh, that phrase, heard at a party, years ago.
A wife walked by and a guy said
"in your dreams, Arnold,"
but we were carrying on, this wife and me, married too.

She would wait by the supermarket in her family
    squareback,
I'd scrunch down next to her to hide from the neighbors
until she closed her garage door and we'd nervously kiss,
talk smalltalk in the kitchen,
and what we lived those days for,
taking each other away from that suburban bedroom,
doing the things you dreamwomen learned from her:

Oh, you love seeing your indulgences
multiply the little money I have to take me to the end,
bring happiness to my kids;
— oh don't stop, not now —
push the mesmerizing fire of cremation away, — yes, yes,
yes, oh, yes —   — oh, yes —

— and her telling me how she was leaving her husband
and me knowing I didn't love her enough to go with her,
yet wanting to love her so I would not be so cruel
to the four of us in her husband's bed, hairs stuck in teeth,
fornicating upside-down, inside-out, bodies like pretzels,

and that unexpected openness I felt the moment
    she stopped
holding civilization together with her bottommuscles;
as she relaxed I knew she was letting go of
her husband, her son, her life-as-she-had-known-it.

Can you possibly pity me lying there,
    her real voids exposed,
me unable to fill them? Can you allow me loneliness
    that moment
I knew forever that adultery doesn't work without love?

So please, before your nightly visits — don't stop —
but briefly behold the limitations of my manhood —

you, her sisters and mothers and daughters,
    you women in my dreams.

HOMECOMING

Nose around the small expensive house.
You open all the shutters, I'll open all the doors.
Has the neighbor-girl kept the dogs fed?
Look, on the patio – at least they have water.

I'll sort quickly through the mail.
Oh I think we're overdrawn, that check didn't clear.
Granta says they're "seriously considering" a story.
And three rejection slips – two for me, one for you.

Never thought I'd miss the dogs so.
Bigger and Terrier are looking old, is that heat-rash?
Puppy Molly has grown again.
I don't feel as bad leaving her, so young.

I'll go out for milk.
What else do the kids need to get through tomorrow?
How does it feel being back?
Is there beer?

Any word from Mom or her nursing home?
Check the answering machine.
The Visa-lady only gave us till the twenty-fifth.
Chit-chat nervous as a couple before a funeral.

AUTOBIOGRAPHICAL INCIDENT
(by Kate Arnold, for a fifth grade assignment)

"Kate and Scotty come here please!" It was Sunday morning, why weren't we going to church? I started to walk to the bedroom with a very young Scotty. At the time he was seven and I was nine. I can feel my grin spreading from ear to ear. Mom's pregnant, I know it. I can't wait for my new baby brother. In the bedroom Mom and Dad were on the bed sitting up. Dad looked older than usual with his frown, his graying and all ready thinned out hair. The last little bit that made him look old was the little pudgy stomach which wasn't small and didn't look like it before you added the too small T-shirt. Mom. Sitting up with her short hair, a white Ann Taylor shirt and blue sweat pants.

"Kids, sit down, I have something to tell you." Something was wrong. Scotty and I sat on the bed. Then they sprang it on us.

"Kids, Daddy and I aren't getting along so well, and we need some time apart, so I'm going to move into a different house." Scotty immediately climbed into Moms lap which I longed for. The was it went was Mom was the comforting one and Dad was the teasing and roughhousing one. I needed the comforting ones right now. I still didn't realize what was going on. I almost started laughing. I needed to laugh. Why now Kate I thought. Why are you

I(Autobiographical Incident continued)

laughing when you just found out your parents aren't going to live with each other? Maybe I was still in shock or maybe nothing important enough happened. One way or the other I don't remember anything else until that night. That night it all started adding up. About three days before I had seen Mom standing against the wall with her stubborn face on. Dad was yelling and then slammed the wall with his hands each hand about six inches away from her head on either side. I wouldn't believe it. I couldn't believe it. After that I tried tried so hard to make myself forget it. I had forgotten it until tonight. From then on I decided to take charge of my own life. They could stay stuck on this separation. It didn't happen just this fast. It took me about two months to adjust and take charge.

    This event changed my whole life, from the beginning people had always been there telling me the separation was for the better. Now Mom and Dad wouldn't have to argue with each other and they can pay more attention to Scotty and I. Even yesterday I was thinking about it. My Mom called me at my Dad's house. She asked to talk to Dad and I said

    "Here Dad, its Mom." That's when it troubled me. I knew they weren't calling to say I love you and when are you coming home. The only reason they were talking was to figure out what they had to.

TO BO

Today, like so many recently,
we have moved closer to living apart.
Your parents have been told.
You have a place now.
We've worked out the finances for a while.
Soon we'll work out a schedule –
it looks like Tuesday nights for Kate,
Saturday mornings for Scotty,
weekends together.

    – Underneath the haunting thought:
       soon may be the last night
       I spend with you

        – I wish I were better at telling you
         how much I love you

            – Illiterate

HERE IN THE KITCHEN

"Oddity wan chocolat,"
Kate will say, mock-seriously.
"Daddity, him vehy tirsty."

I harrumph and rip open a
Carnation's hot chocolate envelope
and zap a cup, with her watching,

then say, mock-serious myself,
"Will Tae bring chocolat to Oddity?"
— Kate waits two beats to tell me I'm pushing it,

then returns to her babytalk,
says, "Oh Tay, Daddity"
and takes the warm drink back to Scotty,

who, playing a computer-game,
not used to his older sister's ministrations,
says "Thank you, Kate,"

not just politely, but with an openness
so straightforward that
I can see his face through walls —

here in the kitchen, where
I'm unloading the dishwasher
and Kate finds me

missing the Mommity, of course,
but this other side of me rejoices,
says This is okay,

God I'm doing O. K.

HOW IT WENT

Friday Evening

You are not with me,
again.
I call the kids and don't ask to speak to you —
that is what you want, I think.

Friday Night

You are not with me.
With new friends, I sing songs in a meadow
We watch for meteor showers.
I almost call back, for you.

Saturday Morning

You are not with me.
Horses pass by in an elaborate city-to-city race.
To finish, they have to climb that slope we stayed by.
You are still sleeping, I'm sure.

SEPARATION

There was no Saxon word for separation,
for the sun rising on my family in one place
and me in another – in this case, our house.
Saxons used words like broken or ripped or torn.
I leave, wander aimlessly through the library,
opening one book, another magazine.
. . . Before Sylvia Plath put her head in the oven
she padded the doors to her children's rooms
and made them snacks for when they awoke.
No-one seems to know why Ted left her,
his wife who was giving sixteen hours a day
to the little family they had formed together,
but was, before she put her head in the oven,
broken, ripped, and torn. On a hunch, I confirm
there was no Saxon word for suicide, either.

TRANSITIONS

I: Overnight at Dad's

Tuesday night, dark as death except for
the digital clock that beams 3:28.
The kids are with my wife, who left nine months ago.
The teachers say they're doing well,
except Scotty, eight, has problems with transitions.

I roll over and remember my recent lower G. I. exam;
this new rite of passage to middle age.
He and that nurse pushing their ninety-foot probe past
a small throbbing hemorrhoid as the nurse says
    "Watch the teevee."
– I still see tiny brown specks like pebbles on a pink path.

< >

Wednesday evening Scotty settles himself at the piano.
Kate, ten, takes me into her room to discuss
what we've never talked about before.
She carefully prints what she wants to say on lined paper:
– "Daddy, if it were me
you'd be all the husband she should need."
I hug her and say "I made mistakes –
we both made a lot of mistakes."

She says "Did you kill anyone?"
She looks at me squarely as if
nothing less would warrant this.
Kate says, "Jesus says we should all forgive.
You know that, Daddy."
I say, "Grownups' lives aren't so simple,"
as Scotty pushes through the door
crying, "Don't leave me out like this!"

< >

— calm them now.
Lie down with them until they doze off.
Then get up, clear the table, start the dishwasher,
finally tumble in with them —
hug one child then the other through the night.

< >

Wednesday night at 4:12 I think about my mistakes.
Jesus called sin "missing the mark."
But scholars are going over the evidence now, the scrolls,
and only a few words can they agree on.
I'll bet "missing the mark" won't make the cut . . . .

(Transitions, continued)

The clock says 4:46 when I start worrying about Scotty —
slow at moving from one thing to another.
We expect so much from these kids
— transitions —
you're never finished with what you're doing
— you're interrupted —
but the toughest thing about transitions
are the wounds you bring to what's next.

At 5:16 I put my arm around lightly-sleeping Kate,
who, thank God, seems to feel safer that way.
There is no doubt she breathes deeper with me there.
Feeling unexpectedly blessed, I draw a deep breath myself,
bone-tired, headed toward sleep.

II: WAITING FOR DAWN

Although Kate and Scotty have their own rooms,
when their mom moved out we all slept in the double bed.
Everyone said this was chancy with a daughter,
so for a while Kate slept by us on a floorpad,
then in her own room, just to the East.

Still my boy sleeps with me.
If I touch him while he's falling asleep
he recoils and I retreat.

Toward morning, though, while it is still dark
an arm or leg or his back touches me.
When I turn and lightly hug him,
Scotty melts to my body like a pillow.

At the first hint of light,
old here-I-come-ready-or-not-dawn,
I loosen from Scotty and think of Kate.
Alone and being to the East, she will have to face it first.
She seems to have been born knowing this.

III: MIDDLE SCHOOL

"Scotty, you wanted me to wake you before I go
    exercise,"
I say at 5:45 to Scotty, in his own room now.
I touch him and he pulls away. "Here, hot chocolate,"
    I say.

At six, jockwomen, stopwatches around their necks,
grind me through lunges, freeweights, crunches,
    and pushups
before we head off to do "stadiums," where we climb the
80 stairs of the bowl. After three trips, I'm sweating,
    breathless.
The bowl gets steeper up high, so the last eighteen steps
    are brutal.

(Transitions, continued)

My heart pounds in my ears, which scares me, but I keep
    going,
and the pause at the top isn't completely unlike orgasm,
hunched over crying for two breaths into my folded arms
only to then look up, out over the waking town I call home
where Kate sleeps and Scotty fiddles with his math.

< >

When I get back, Scotty is at the piano.
"Homework done?" I ask.
He returns to the coffee table where he's working.
I make sure Kate is up and pour myself some grapefruit
    juice.
When she joins me I say "good morning," and she glares,
then says, "Please tell me you didn't wear those shorts,"
and I look down at my blowsy old neon-pink-and-azure
    bathing suit.
"Guilty," I say with a smile, "but I finally did five stadiums."
"Dad, you're absolutely hopeless," she says.

I tell Scotty even if he isn't through he has to gather his
    books
and brush his teeth. "When Kate wants to leave, she can,"
    I say.
Now that they ride bikes, Scotty knows he's lost his old
    power to make us wait for him — he stuffs his backpack.
"And your teeth," I say, and he heads back to the
    bathroom.

< >

That's about it. They join the kids pedaling toward middle
    school.
Scotty's in choir and Kate's taken up guitar: music abounds.
By now they are at school and it's like the view after
I reached the top of the stadium: almost unbearable
    pain,
then an unexpected vista. Sometimes everything aches,
but my heart, my heart, my heart has held.

PONYTAIL

The teacher puts our chairs in a circle—
he wants us to go deeper and
I want to understand my sadness.
Outside the window a young girl,
preparing for a dance class,
removes her blouse, and ties it around her leotard.
If she knew I was watching she would not lift her arms so
as she brushes her hair, or at least
she would lower her elbows so I couldn't
gaze at her as, handful by handful,
she creates a ponytail.
Her light-brown eyes hold not a care as we
huddle in this thoughtful circle,
carefully coached to face our pain, our poems.
She could not know the sensuality of a ponytail—
how it lays demurely on a horse or a zebra
but sometimes, with a quick swish,
lifts to reveal the darkness of my dreams.

Graceful girls in leotards don't change as I age
—they are promise made flesh—
yet the fantasy of their caresses fades.

I love this teacher as no other man,
desire to be part of his circle—
but look, she is stretching now,
touching both arms to a leg.
How can I be sad here, surrounded by miracles?

DIVORCE ALBUMS

At my bookstore
next to the wedding books are divorce books
to capture forever lingerie from secret dates.
A special section for the growing list of lies.

A disintegration chapter for
the Christmas cards not sent,
the children's lunches un-prepared,
the little blowups that infect the house,

with a place for the counselers' and lawyers' bills
and the real-estate commission statements
and photographs of the couple
in various stages of exhaustion, longing, even hate,

an entire section for the day the kids are told
Pictures capturing their fractured faces
as their lives are changed dramatically –
the two who brought them forth are irreconcilable

The planet provides leather-binding and gold-stamping
of books for those who reconcile,
wide publicity for the smiling faces
of those who beat the odds

and the others always have their
wedding and divorce books side by side.
The wedding may have been for the parents but
the particulars of a divorce –

the scarred children held in the middle of the night,
the unexpected moments of cruelty and tenderness,
the end of this they began together,
this is theirs alone.

A WAVE STARTS AS A SWELL

or the start of a swell,
or the start of a start of a swell,
then grows as our love did, Bo, until –
well what a wave does is confront
the remains of prior waves
planes over what is left until it suddenly
crashes –
that moment painters paint,
sometimes with a deadening thunder,
yet the wave does not die but rolls on,
a similar-but-diminished life,
a brine wave that confronts
previous brine waves until it
laps up on one rocky shore or another
and finally scuttles itself under new waves,
perhaps gives itself to a growing undertow –
remember how we used to warn the kids?

SEPARATED

In the cool evenings of this altitude,
when I go out on the deck
at the tail end of a divorce,
the mountains seem to know
nothing's turned out as I planned.

Yesterday I broke down when a poet revealed what
she had to do to escape her own father.
Pain in other people's lives seems unbearable.
The pain in my own life is too, and
I can't afford to cry very often.

I'm glad I wept yesterday among friends.
I must find a way to gather these mountains
and carry them with me.
I want to learn how to love.

MY SON'S SEX

In my dream my son had met this girl,
 I saw them touching,
so I had to tell him everything at once:
the times you do it when you shouldn't,
the times you don't do it when you should;
the shame when you show desire only
to have her tell you,
in no uncertain terms, that you are acting inappropriately,
the *hard-walled loneliness* of that;
the times when sex and love lay upon one another
not just as concentric circles but as the same circle exactly,
the times they aren't even in the same room together,
can't even shout through walls at one another,
yet sex still shouts;

how sex shadows every human interaction,
even between a child like himself and his teachers,
his mother, even his father, me; the way
sex has colored his thinking as long as he can remember,
how sex separated his mother from me,
how it's brought him to wear his bathing suit
in the bathtub;
the way the women know they have it to give,
or is that wrong,

do we just keep imploring them, or is all that changing;
the way those questions rattle around in the houses
    of our beings;
how if you include homosexual love there is no end to it,
sex propels everything; even my solitary blind mother,
his grandmother in the nursing home, is shaped by it;
the road he is about to start down has no exit –
but I wake up then, realize my son is only eleven,
I won't say these things to him now, nor probably ever –
to say things like this in real life it is always too early
    or too late.

THEY'RE SURE I WAS NEVER YOUNG

"Just listen through to the third song,"
I say, when the kids realize
I've slipped my Judy Collins CD
between Save Ferris and Shania Twain.

I keep the kids' hands
from the car's CD player
while Judy sings words like
"Everyone's singing I've got to be me
—without you,"

about a time gone by, yet,
since their Mom has moved
to another town with another man,
a time still here.

On the second track, Judy sings
"I love you, I love you,
The first time I saw you,
and I always will love you Marie."

They chide me about Judy's
naked pictures on the jacket,
and tell me, of all my geezer favorites
—James Taylor, Bonnie Raitt, Willie Nelson—

Judy, whose photos reveal a body that,
even then, wasn't seventeen—
Judy's the worst.

I make them listen to the third cut:
her ironic, "you're coming back,
you're running back, to happy endings,
just a minor bending, a happy end."

A WAY TO MEASURE YOURSELF

You can only displace so much water.

Fill the tub until water spills into the overflow,
then twist your legs until the knees are covered.

Conditioning won't help, if you are a good parent
or bad artist it won't matter.

If you have a penis, hold it down with your hand,
or breasts, ditto, as you submerge the chest.

Peek, at the last minute, for any knee-islands,
bring full breath into the lungs,

and, concentrating on the knees,
gently drop your head under.

That is your high-water mark,
you can do no more.

Part 2
JOHNNA

SLEEPING FATHER

His toddler, of the new family,
sleeps better this week.
One soft "Mama" around midnight,
nothing more.

Twelve-year-old Johnna stirs on the couch.
Quietly, but enough to wake her father.
Years before, after he left her mom,
she would awaken the household,
yelling "Don't!"

He's alert now, in the dim light of dawn,
up on one elbow, straining to hear.

But the only sound now
is the padding of paws on wood.
He didn't close the kitchen door
and the dog runs free.

FIRST WIFE

That summer before we separated,
I talked her into tennis lessons
she learned forehands, backhands, and volleys.

Afterwards I hit balls to her,
gentle, soft shots that lured her slowly to the net,
where, with sudden firmness I hit the ball past her.

Until then I would compliment her strokes
and call lines in her favor,
the kindest opponent in the world.

EARLY MORNING, AMHERST

Soon after I set foot in
 Emily Dickinson's garden
 a sleepy guard appears
—I've been watching she says
You've been careful but
Underneath there are bulbs—

We make adjustments and I
wait for my daughter to give her command
when she's ready to snap the shutter.

She wants to master the limitations
of this large-format camera her college loaned her.
It loves light and stillness, she says,
capturing motion with the sun low is
the worst use of its gift
but if you jolt the flower
at just the right moment, Dad,
we might capture a
water-droplet in mid-air

(Early Morning, Amherst, continued)

I wait silently
while the garden-guard watches us,
arms folded. Johnna's face is
hidden by a black cloth over her camera.

I say, One false move and we're dead meat
She says Hush
And finally Now! Hit it now!

JAPANESE GRAVEYARD ON KAUAI

One afternoon I drove Johnna way past Kappa,
deep into desolate cane-hauling roads.
We came upon an old graveyard on a hill near the ocean.
Before the tall cane it had overlooked the Pacific.

I got out, trying to convey my wonder
    to my young daughter.
The wooden markers, in Japanese with a little English,
marked the lives of turn-of-the-century fishing families.
I coaxed her out of the car and we walked
to one grave, then another.
One had fresh flowers, but most were overgrown.
I told her about once-prosperous fishing fleets,
gone now. She stood silent.

This is all that's left,
I told her at one family's grave,
after the tortuous trip from Japan,
after building the fishing fleet,
after extracting an honest living from the sea,
after constructing villages—
they're tourist towns today, I said.
No words from her as we returned to the car.

(Japanese Graveyard on Kauai, continued)

I said I hoped we had more left than that
even though I'd moved away from her mother
and watched her so silent, next to me in
the rental car dwarfed by the sugar cane.

I kept looking over at my small passenger who
wore a cotton skirt over her bathing suit,
peeking up at her father out at the edge of somewhere.
Her eyes said what can he teach me but chaos?

THE ART OPENING

Our daughter Johnna has won three photography awards,
so my ex-wife and I treat her and her artist-friends
to a fancy dinner after an opening in San Francisco.
We sit one person apart, my ex-wife's husband
on the other side of her, subdued in a tie and tweed jacket.
Johnna sits between us,
little conversation bits filled with double meanings
    pass around her,
take her parents back, *despite our differences we have done*
    one thing well,
and my bruised heel/fallen arch doesn't bother at all.
Johnna, often shy, seems oblivious to her aging mother
    and father
tonight, she is radiant in her moment, she has survived,
two of the show's sponsors will buy her oversized
black-and-white triptychs, so unexpectedly bold,
for more money than she spends in a month.
I bask in her reflected glory until we realize
the parking lot is closing just as desert arrives
so I have to ransom the car, and I can't get my loafers
    back on.

(The Art Opening, continued)

Why did I wear new shoes with this foot?
Johnna walks with me, supports my arm.
The cold San Francisco blow hard, and every step hurts.
I hobble like that, my ex- and her husband in his tweeds,
smoothly ahead,
and realize I am celebrating my daughter's success before
mine ever happened; I picture an airport,
me gunning my plane –
I realize there's not enough runway for me
to get airborne.
I lean almost all my weight on Johnna now, shivering.

Part 3
PARENTS

MY PARENTS BEFORE ME

This photograph of them courting in Charleston,
the Dartmouth man sent south by GE before the war,
a dark suit with a touch of white handkerchief,
her gloves held in her left hand, she looks
unfettered, far from her mother on the farm
downing pills by the handful.
Her swaying curvehugging beads, caught in mid-sway,
give no hint she will follow in her mother's footsteps,
her care will become his life—
just this snappy couple stepping out.

DAD'S KNIGHTS

I didn't choose a good year to beat you at chess,
didn't know what trouble you were in,
you with those slashing knights,
but who paid little attention to the openings.
You never accepted that unless you open up the
queen's side she'll never sweep across that long diagonal,
change every relationship on the board.

Now your hopeful yellow alligator shirt hangs in my closet.
I wish I'd argued with you that year,
pointed my young finger to chess books that said
you have to develop the other pieces—
knights can't do it alone.

MAVERICK

Harry will never forget the moment he first believed
he was born in God, part of a plan so intricate
he could never describe it to anyone.
That Friday he forgave Billy for tripping him
 in the bushes and kicking him –
all was forgiven that day. He was on the path,
and with each breath he let God

      hold him

the way he'd held that stuffed animal when he got home,
that limp lamb he'd found when his dog Maverick got out.
He'd found the lamb in the attic after a car had killed his dog
Maverick and carried it around the house for weeks.

When he came home from the bushes he held the lamb
and started yelling at his mother –Why couldn't she have
been there and told Billy he'd been sick, that Harry had
been in a coma, near death—yet that Friday he knew

      no one ever dies—

he was forgiven for yelling at his mother.
And knew after Billy was punished he'd be forgiven too.

(Maverick, continued)

Forgiveness would be like air.
Maverick was in heaven or on his way.
All things happen at once,
and the joy Harry found at twelve
is part of him (though it fades so easily)
Harry knows joy should be now,
can be for ever and forever and ever.

HOOKY

Mom's out of Elgin hospital, helping me play hooky.
She buys me a mint-chocolate milkshake.
Her face is so calm after these dryings-out,
her eyes follow my every word as if I were a poet.

MY FATHER'S EYES

Still I see my father's eyes
across formica from me,
after I told him I would no longer deny
my mother's alcoholism.

They seemed to get glassier
in his seventy-fifth year.
He asked me, from his heart,
why I couldn't forgive.

We both watched his hands shake
still I held my ground,
mentioning four drinks a night,
detailing pills.

He said, son it is the high point of her day
Don't deny her happy hour.
Suddenly, unexpected tears,
and him drawing his handkerchief

in that harsh California sunlight I had brought him to,
bringing the white cloth
slowly to his face,
lightly blowing his nose,

rubbing his eyes while I admitted
I was changing my part in our family game
pretty late in life—
he whispered, a Christian should forgive.

My mind jumped to the truths I wouldn't tell him
I was jealous of his loyalty
 (though self-help books had other names for it)
to this woman who had formed his life,

my mother, and because,
old, glassy-eyed and shaking,
he had courage enough to confront me,
care enough to cry.

FALLING

Great, Mom, the day I arrive for the poetry week
you, blind, break your hip in the nursing home.
    I learn this from Sybil, who calls from Tulsa
    just so I know what's going on, she says,
    and hints I should drive back to the bay area,
    stand by you for the operation.
    I ask the time of the accident,
    and she allows it was right after your
    doctor-prescribed drink.
    I do not remind her of your previous falls.
    She asks again where I will be for your birthday Friday,
    and I tell her, for the fifth time, we'll have to celebrate
        late.
If Dad were alive and here today
he would tear down route 80 to be with you.
You must have died inside, yourself, Mom
last Christmas when you couldn't wake him
to take you to the bathroom at Sybil's house,
    and I know he always had carpets in case you fell.
    In the nursing home I put you in afterwards,
        they don't.
    I never asked them to install carpets for you
    although you wanted me to.
    On linoleum, even this slight fall broke your hip.
    This afternoon they'll insert a pin
    and I'll be up at this poetry deal,

    which I'll admit doesn't make much sense,
      fooling around with verse when the rest of the world
      has moved on to multi-media and any one
          with the talent
      of the people here could be making money,
          not paying it,
      big money but we're not TV writers, we're poets,
      and as you probably guessed
      I'm not completely at home here either,
      although more so than usual,
      sometimes, Mom, much more at home than usual.
Yes, even Dad was disappointed I wrote poetry.
But I swear he knew he was going to die on that trip,
and when I last saw him he asked for a tape of my reading,
so when they handed me the plastic baggy
    of his personal effects
three items: his wallet, keys, and the recording
of my reading at the tiny bookstore in San Jose,
where they clapped for me, like they meant it.
Mom, poetry will not make me an awful father
    and husband
like your mother said it did to Poe.
I would give you the tape if you asked
It would play in that Recordings for the Blind machine,
I checked.

(Falling, continued)

> I take a breath and call you at the hospital
> where you're not at all a mean ogre, but this new
> honestly-open self you've been with your new
>   roommate—
> you're the mother I'd always wanted you to be.
> We've had a reckoning when we least expected it,
> haven't we Mom?

You don't ask me to come down but tell me
the last thing you wanted to do was ruin my vacation,
but you never ask about the poetry week,
what we do here, or why—I ask about the operation:
the break, the anesthetic, the pin.
And about your roommate, who's had the operation
   before.
I tell you I love you.
When you don't respond I tell you
I wish I could be with you, I really do.
I would hold your hand and tell you how strong
   your heart is,
and you would smile, which I don't think you do
when I mouth the words into the phone.

If you'd asked I'd have told you
we write all the time up here, a new poem every day
and mornings we share them with each other,
say what works and what doesn't.
I like the poets more all the time,
and you have me thinking about why we're here,
our sensibilities, and I wonder if one or two of the
    others
has a parent like you: someone tough to come
    to terms with
who keeps us going back to our typewriters,
back to the root of our thinking, words,
trying to create an order,
even one that lasts for a stanza or two
because that is one of the few things we get
when we're falling; oh, maybe we earn a few bucks,
have lovers, maybe raise kids
but you're talking real luck when people clap
    for your poems,
and even though we keep falling
toward the nursing home with the hard floor
we keep writing
because outside of family there is little else
falling toward home, falling toward death,
all falling backward toward our own beginnings.

HARRY'S SONG

The flight from South Carolina is overbooked—
Harry insists they volunteer for the fifteen hundred dollars
    offered
if they'll wait and go later.
He has to watch the money now.
Where will his mother live?
And, immediately, should he let her drink on the plane?

    At the last minute there is room for everybody:
    they upgrade Harry's family to first class.
    Harry thinks this is a good omen,
        and when the flight attendant,
    one of those graceful women from whom a southern
        accent sounds right,
    offers condolences (she must know from the
        bereavement fares)
    he feels a miracle is possible.
    That's what will be needed to take care of his mom,
        a miracle.

    After free drinks, his mother sleeps. At the funeral
        his mom said
    his dad didn't want to be buried with his own
        Yankee kin,
    because they never loved him enough. His wife reads.

Regarding the hereafter, Harry could still hear
    his dad say
When I die I'm going to Florence,
and now he is there, Harry has done his duty,
his father is at rest under moss-dripping trees.

Harry looks out to a lumbering wing.
Huge planes fly just from air over that elliptical shape.
Think of that, flying.
This is his first quiet since his father died
    three days ago,
and words come to him.
He speaks the words silently, then softly.
He grabs the airsick bag and writes them down:

    From the top
    as my head balds and my belly rounds
    I'm becoming a perfect airfoil.
    My hands at my sides –
    when the wind is right I'll cup them and take off,
    nimble as a sports car.
    Look, up in the sky.
    Watch for me.

His mother snores, and the plane drones on.
Things seem eternally still.
He folds the bag and puts it in his pocket.

SHAKING

Seconds ticked on (two, five),
offices no longer safe,
my window bowing like plastic (ten),
I needed shelter (fifteen),
spotted a desk across the hall,

dove underneath, someone already there,
a large woman filling the entire space;
my head by her bottom (twenty),
sprinklerheads falling from the ceiling,
when it ended (twenty-three) we giggled.

Later my little family unhurt,
our house undamaged, just power out.
We put our candles away and
headed for my parents' small apartment,
my extended family, two by two by two.

Perhaps I knew then, watching my mother,
her party self after cocktails,
and my dad, temporary patriarch.
perhaps I knew he would die, soon,
with as little warning as an earthquake.

He found this never-used two-foot flashlight
and together we inserted batteries.
I enjoyed a wonderful well-fathered moment
as it shone its first light
in this emergency explicable to anyone.

But soon the aftershocks started,
damned things, more earthquakes really, and
reports, how close we'd come to complete c\h/a\o/s,
people building new foundations under old houses,
and new shaking, day or night.

Whatever we were doing, we'd run to the children,
hold them, then, quick, turn on teevee.
Where's the epi-center? What's the Richter reading?

The next week a friend called saying
children from alcoholic families
were particularly hard hit. I said not me,
I'm o\k/a\y.

SOFTBALL

I

In the mountains on a company outing,
no reason to worry about anything,
but Harry's mind is in the valley.
His boss winced this morning,
probably at something Harry said –
hiking along a trail Harry suddenly
shouts No! from deep within,
loud enough for others to hear,
but they are caught up in the way
the trees change with the altitude,
and how the flowers that have lost
petals are still beautiful.

II

The last part of the outing is softball
Driving to it, soe idiot rides his bumper
Harry knows how to handle her:
at fifty miles an hour he hits his barkes,
watchers her careen to the shoulder,
swerve back into traffic, accelerate,
and cut him off. Through the sunroof,
she gives Harry the finger.

III

Harry thinks his boss,
a thin tennis player,
organizes this softball game
to be one of the boys.
The boss plays third base,
the captain of the other team.
Harry, in his frist at-bath,
keeps looking over at him,
and strikes out.

But the second time
he manages to hit past the infield.
Harry rounds first base, and second,
decides to go for it,
short of breath runs for third;
his boss catches the ball
in front of him.
How easily he could tag Harry out,
but he magically turns the wront way,
doesn't make the play, yells safe,
something Harry's father never did,
nor most men.

(Softball, continued)

Harry is angry
this man has seen through him,
yet he suddenly relaxes,
sees a secretary at the plate;
she's choked up on the bat like
this is her one chance
to pound the hell out of something
and Harry shortens his lead
so he can watch: the overgrown
outfield so green this time of year;
how the pitcher sets, then throws
and springs off the mound
to be ready for a batted ball
in this once-a-year
middle-aged softball game;
these people so like himself,
this is the only life he has.

Part 4

and Beyond

Scotty and Kate celebrate her start at Med School in September, 2009

FREE, FLY, BACK, BREAST

The six-and-unders sit in numbered chairs,
then hold hands in a daisy-chain
to walk to the proper lane with their team's coach
and stand nervously until the horn sounds,
when they get to splash in and make arm-windmills.
I, the false-start judge, see it all—
their legs that don't contribute much,
and the way they brush the lane-markers
and breathe too often so it seems to take forever.
Still they all finish and how they beam as they climb out!

. . . as the seven-eights take their places at the start
and at the horn dive straighter out,
stroke with more authority.
My Scotty-boy, normally no star, cuts five seconds off
    his best time.
And they don't breathe—coach says, after today
you'll have all fall to breathe.
The nine-tens don't hold hands but walk out knowing
this is the combined meet—all the teams are here
Sure-footed Kate slips in her starting dive
and never recovers,
trying to keep up with the eleven-twelves,
who really clip along.

(Free, Fly, Back, Breast continued)

But it's the thirteen-and-unders who take
    your breath away.
They seem to cover the pool in five strokes,
their parents who've shuttled them for years
beaming over this transition from summer to fall,
childhood to adulthood—
this communal concentration on a good start.

CARPACCIO

Wine was already spilled on the pink tablecloth,
the two couples' cheeks already flushed,
but she hadn't noticed,
so when her husband split a shrimp cocktail with Bill's wife,
she surprised herself by joining with Bill to split carpaccio.

The raw beef came laid out like a flower,
deep red petals on bone plate.

Bill spread capers and minced onions wantonly,
and didn't worry about seeds as he squeezed the lemon.

She could feel his hunger as he gathered the beef,
then, his fork still in his left hand,
took a large red chunk into his mouth;
from next to him she felt she could taste
onionpungent and lemonsour and capersalt—
despite herself she could taste them
merging on his tongue with the cool red flesh;

then in front of God and everybody in the nice restaurant,
in front of their shrimp-cocktail-eating spouses,
lifting her fork over the spilled wine,
she followed Bill's brazen lead.

DANCING AT HALLOWEEN

All parts of love are here with us
as we ask one another to dance,
the women so festive in Halloween garb—
one tribal princess, several bats, a slinky disco woman,
and of course plump pumpkins, perky cowgirls.

Filial love abounds as we all smile too much,
chit-chatting about each other's children
and the price of real estate in the valley we overlook.

Erotic love taps our shoulders as the singer croons.
A few men still pose as predators,
    but most are cautious now,
single at midlife, and the women, comfortable
in their lonely bodies, know what they have to share.

Agape love is here too, forgiving errant dance steps
and premature marriages,
    blessing the few souls not dancing now
and those like me, making outdated movements
on the dance floor with one of the pumpkins.
I want to tell her that my new love, far away tonight,
is here with us too. The music slows and
the singer/disk jockey, portable mike in hand,
walks onto the dance floor and serenades us.
She leans in to me. It is time to go home.

INVITATION TO THE OPERA

They say to handle each paper once,
but I can never do that with opera invites,
for I am someone who would like to like opera.
So when one comes, along with the bills,
fundraising letters from my daughter's pricey college,
small magazines that published my work—
magazines I keep renewing but never find time to read,
even gold-embossed credit-card offerings to my ex-wife,
it's the opera offer I can't throw away.

It would be so good if I could get my daughter to go.
I wonder whether to subscribe or just pick one or two.
Perhaps start with a familiar name:
La Traviata, Madame Butterfly, Aida, or *Carmen.*
Or how about these colorful ads for the new ones:
The Death of Klinghoffer or *Nixon in China*—
any program that puts the stars in tails and flowing gowns.
Some Wednesday, Friday, or Saturday, maybe next year
I'll be there, part of the daringly dressed audience
as the lights dim. Imagine me in that heart-stopping
quiet just before the songs echo into the night.

AT JASPER RIDGE RANCH

She's teaching me about horses,
how you hang their halters
next to the stalls in case of fire,
and English saddles—almost bareback—
are not just frou frou but the only way
a horse can jump.
She says rhythmically moving
up and down on a horse
is like making love to a woman.
Perhaps, I think, a woman
you're not in love with
but I am not yet a horseman.

ABOUT THE AUTHOR:

Kevin Arnold has published more than fifty poems in the *Seattle Review*, the *California Poetry Journal*, and *The Beloit Fiction Journal* and similar literary magazines. One of his short stories, excerpted from his novel *The Sureness of Horses*, won first place at the 2009 San Francisco Book Festival.

Kevin received a Master of Fine Arts in Creative Writing from San Jose State University in 2007. He is the president of Poetry Center San Jose, with headquarters in the historic home of California poet Edwin Markham. PCSJ is the parent organization of the California Poets Festival and the national literary journal *Caesura*.

A U. S. Navy veteran and equestrian, Kevin is an Elder in the Presbyterian Church, USA. He's currently serving on the Grand Jury of Santa Clara County.

See more, including his blog at:
http://www.redroom.com/author/kevin-arnold

www.ingramcontent.com/pod-product-compliance
Lightning Source LLC
Chambersburg PA
CBHW071835290426
44109CB00017B/1826